MEDI

SOLITARY WALKER

Jean-Jacques Rousseau

Meditations of a Solitary Walker

Translated by Peter France

PENGUIN BOOKS

PENGUIN BOOKS

Published by the Penguin Group

Penguin Books USA Inc., 375 Hudson Street,
New York, New York 10014, U.S.A.
Penguin Books Ltd, 27 Wrights Lane,
London W8 5TZ, England
Penguin Books Australia Ltd, Ringwood,
Victoria, Australia
Penguin Books Canada Ltd, 10 Alcorn Avenue,
Toronto, Ontario, Canada M4V 3B2
Penguin Books (N.Z.) Ltd, 182–190 Wairau Road,
Auckland 10, New Zealand

Penguin Books Ltd, Registered Offices:
Harmondsworth, Middlesex, England

Published in Penguin Books 1995

These selections are from Peter France's translation of *Reveries of the Solitary Walker*, published by Penguin Books.

ISBN 0 14 60.0194 X

Printed in the United States of America

MEDITATIONS OF A
SOLITARY WALKER

First Walk

So now I am alone in the world, with no brother, neighbour or friend, nor any company left me but my own. The most sociable and loving of men has with one accord been cast out by all the rest. With all the ingenuity of hate they have sought out the cruellest torture for my sensitive soul, and have violently broken all the threads that bound me to them. I would have loved my fellow-men in spite of themselves. It was only by ceasing to be human that they could forfeit my affection. So now they are strangers and foreigners to me; they no longer exist for me, since such is their will. But I, detached as I am from them and from the whole world, what am I? This must now be the object of my inquiry. Unfortunately, before setting out on this quest, I must glance rapidly at my present situation, for this is a necessary stage on the road that leads from them to myself.

After the fifteen years or more that this strange state of affairs has lasted, I still imagine that I am suffering from indigestion and dreaming a bad dream, from which I shall wake with my pain gone to find myself once again in the midst of my friends. Yes, I must surely have slipped unwittingly from waking into sleep, or rather from life into death. Wrenched somehow out of the natural order, I have been plunged into an incomprehensible chaos where I can make nothing out, and the more I think about my present situation, the less I can understand what has become of me.

How indeed could I ever have foreseen the fate that lay in wait for me? How can I envisage it even today, when I have succumbed to it? Could I, in my right mind, suppose that I, the very same man who I was then and am still today, would be taken beyond all doubt for a monster, a poisoner, an assassin, that I would become the horror of the human race, the laughing-stock of the rabble, that all the recognition I would receive from passers-by would be to be spat upon, and that an entire generation would of one accord take pleasure in burying me alive? At the time of this amazing transformation, my instinctive reaction was one of consternation. My emotion and indignation plunged me into a fever which has taken all of ten years to abate, and during this time, as I lurched from fault to fault, error to error, and folly to folly, my imprudent behaviour provided those who control my fate with weapons which they have most skilfully used to settle my destiny irrevocably.

For a long time I put up a resistance as violent as it was fruitless. Being without guile, without skill, without cunning and without prudence, frank, open, impatient and impulsive, I only enmeshed myself further in my efforts to be free, and constantly gave them new holds on me which they took good care not to neglect. But realizing eventually that all my efforts were in vain and my self-torment of no avail, I took the only course left to me, that of submitting to my fate and ceasing to fight against the inevitable. This resignation has made up for all my trials by the peace of mind it brings me, a peace of mind incompatible with the unceasing exertions of a struggle as painful as it was unavailing.

One other thing has contributed to this peaceful state of mind. In all the ingenuity of their hate, my persecutors were led by their animosity to overlook one detail; they forgot the need for a gradation of effects which would have allowed them to be constantly reviving and renewing my pain with some new torment. If they had been clever enough to leave me some glimmer of hope, they would still have a hold on me. They would still be able to lure me with false bait, play with me and then plunge me yet again into the torment of thwarted expectations. But they have already used every weapon at their disposal; by stripping me of everything, they have left themselves unarmed. The weight of slander, contempt, derision and opprobrium that they have heaped on me can no more be increased than it can be relieved; I am as incapable of avoiding it as they are of intensifying it. They were so eager to fill up my cup of misery that neither the power of men nor the stratagems of hell can add one drop to it. Even physical suffering would take my mind off my misfortunes rather than adding to them. Perhaps the cries of pain would save me the groans of unhappiness, and the laceration of my body would prevent that of my heart.

What have I to fear now that there is nothing more to be done? Since they can make things no worse for me, they can no longer alarm me. They have finally set me free from all the evils of anxiety and apprehension; in this at least I can find some consolation. Actual misfortunes have little effect on me; it is easy for me to accept those which I suffer in reality, but not those which I fear. My fevered imagination builds them up, works on them, magnifies them and inspects them from every angle. They are far more of a torment to me imminent than present; the threat is far worse than the blow. As soon as they happen, they lose all the terrors lent to them by imagination and appear in their true size. I find them far less formidable than I had feared, and even in the midst of my suffering I feel a sort of relief. In this state, freed from all further fear and from the anxieties of hope, I shall learn from mere habit to accept ever more easily a situation which can grow no worse; and as my awareness of it is dulled by time they can find no further way of reviving it. So much good my persecutors have done me by recklessly pouring out all the shafts of their hatred. They have deprived themselves of any power over me and henceforward I can laugh at them.

It is not yet two months since a total calm returned to my heart. I had long been without fear, but I continued to hope, and this hope, being alternately encouraged and dashed, was a hold by which a thousand different passions kept me in a state of constant agitation. A recent event as sad as it was unexpected has finally extinguished this feeble ray of hope and shown me that my earthly destiny is irrevocably fixed for all time. Since then I have resigned myself utterly and recovered my peace of mind.

As soon as I began to glimpse the plot in all its ramifications, I lost for ever all notions of changing the public's idea of me during my lifetime; indeed such a change would in future be useless to me since it could no longer be reciprocal. My fellow-men might return to me, but I should no longer be there to meet them. Such is the disdain they have inspired in me that I should find their company tedious and even burdensome, and I am a hundred times happier in my solitude than I could be if I lived among them. They have torn from my heart all the pleasures of society. These can no longer spring up again at my age; it is too late. Let them henceforth do me good or evil, all their actions are indifferent to me, and whatever they may do, my contemporaries will always be as nothing in my eyes.

But I was still counting on the future, and I hoped that a better generation, examining more closely both the judgement pronounced against me by the present generation and its conduct towards me, would find it easy to unravel the stratagems of those who control it and would at last see me as I really am. This was the hope that made me write my *Dialogues* and inspired me with a host of crazy schemes to transmit them to posterity. This hope, distant as it was, kept my soul in the same agitated state as when I was still in search of one just man in the present age, and even if I projected my dreams far into the future, they made me no less a plaything of the men of today. I have explained in the *Dialogues* on what I based this hope. I was mistaken. Fortunately I have realized this soon enough to enjoy before I die a brief period of complete calm and absolute tranquillity. This period began at the time I have mentioned and I have reason to believe that it will continue without interruption.

Hardly a day passes without some new reflections which impress on me how wrong I was to expect the public to change its mind about me even in some future age, since it is guided in its behaviour towards me by mentors who constantly succeed one another in the corporations which have come to hate me. Individuals may die, but not corporate bod-

5

ies. The same passions live on and their violent hatred, as immortal as the demon that inspires it, remains as active as ever. When all my individual enemies are dead there will still be the doctors and Oratorians, and even if these two bodies were my only persecutors, I can be sure that they would no more leave my memory in peace when I die than my person when I am alive. Perhaps with the passage of time the doctors, whom I really did offend, will relent, but the Oratorians, whom I loved, honoured, trusted and never offended, the Oratorians, who are churchmen and well-nigh monks, will remain eternally implacable; since it is their own iniquity which makes a criminal of me, their vanity will never pardon me, and the public, whose animosity they will assiduously keep alight, will remain as implacable as they are.

Everything is finished for me on this earth. Neither good nor evil can be done to me by any man. I have nothing left in the world to fear or hope for, and this leaves me in peace at the bottom of the abyss, a poor unfortunate mortal, but as unmoved as God himself.

Everything external is henceforth foreign to me. I no longer have any neighbours, fellow-men or brothers in this world. I live here as in some strange planet on to which I have fallen from the one I knew. All around me I can recognize nothing but objects which afflict and wound my heart, and I cannot look at anything that is close to me or round about me without discovering some subject for indignant scorn or painful emotion. Let me therefore detach my mind from these afflicting sights; they would only cause me pain, and to no end. Alone for the rest of my life, since it is only in myself that I find consolation, hope and peace of mind, my only remaining duty is towards myself and this is all I desire. This is my state of mind as I return to the rigorous and sincere self-examination that I formerly called my *Confessions*. I am devoting my last days to studying myself and preparing the account which I shall shortly have to render. Let me give myself over entirely to the pleasure of conversing with my soul, since this is the only pleasure that men cannot take away from me. If by meditating on my inner life I am able to order it better and remedy the faults that may remain there, my meditations will not be entirely in vain, and although I am now good for nothing on this earth, I shall not have totally wasted my last days. The free hours of my daily walks have often been filled with delightful contemplations which I am sorry to have forgotten. Such reflections as I have in future I shall preserve in writing; every time I read them they will recall my original pleasure. Thinking of the prize my heart deserved, I shall forget my misfortunes, my persecutors and my disgrace.

These pages will be no more than a formless record of my reveries. I myself will figure largely in them, because a solitary person inevitably thinks a lot about himself. But all the other thoughts which pass through my mind will also have their place here. I shall say what I have thought just as it came to me, with as little connection as the thoughts of this morning have with those of last night. But on the other hand I shall gain new knowledge of my nature and disposition from knowing what feelings and thoughts nourish my mind in this strange state. These pages may therefore be regarded as an appendix to my *Confessions*, but I do not give them this title, for I no longer feel that I have anything to say that could justify it. My heart has been purified in the crucible of adversity and the most careful self-examination can hardly find any remaining traces of reprehensible inclinations. What could I have still to confess when all earthly affections have been uprooted? I have no more reason now to praise than to condemn myself: henceforward I am of no importance among men, and this is unavoidable since I no longer have any real relationship or true companionship with them. No longer able to do good which does not turn to evil, no longer able to act without harming others or myself, my only duty now is to abstain, and this I do with all my heart. But though my body is idle, my mind remains active and continues to produce feelings and thoughts, indeed its inner moral life seems to have grown more intense with the loss of all earthly or temporal interests. My body is now no more than an obstacle and a hindrance to me, and I do all I can to sever my ties with it in advance.

Such an exceptional situation is certainly worth examining and describing, and it is to this task that I am devoting my last days of leisure. To accomplish it successfully I ought to proceed with order and method, but such an undertaking is beyond me, and indeed it would divert me from my true aim, which is to give an account of the successive variations of my soul. I shall perform upon myself the sort of operation that physicists conduct upon the air in order to discover its daily fluctuations. I shall take the barometer readings of my soul, and by doing this accurately and repeatedly I could perhaps obtain results as reliable as theirs. However, my aim is not so ambitious. I shall content myself with keeping a record of my readings without trying to reduce them to a system. My enterprise is like Montaigne's, but my motive is entirely different, for he wrote his essays only for others to read, whereas I am writing down my reveries for myself alone. If, as I hope, I retain the same disposition of mind in my extreme old age, when the time of my departure draws near, I shall recall in reading them the pleasure I have in writing them and by thus reviving times past I shall as it were double the space of my existence. In spite of men I shall still enjoy the charms of company, and in my decrepitude I shall live with my earlier self as I might with a younger friend.

I wrote my first *Confessions* and my *Dialogues* in a continual anxiety about ways of keeping them out of the grasping hands of my persecutors and transmitting them if possible to future generations. The same anxiety no longer torments me as I write this, I know it would be useless, and the desire to be better known to men has died in my heart, leaving me profoundly indifferent to the fate both of my true writings and of the proofs of my innocence, all of which have perhaps already been destroyed for ever. Let men spy on my actions, let them be alarmed at these papers, seize them, suppress them, falsify them, from now on it is all the same to me. I neither hide them nor display them. If they are taken from me during my lifetime, I shall not lose the pleasure of having written them, nor the memory of what they contain, nor the solitary meditations which inspired them and whose source will never dry up as long as I live. If from the moment of my first disasters I had been able to refrain from resisting my fate and had taken the course I am taking now, all the efforts of men and all their terrible machinations would have left me unmoved, and they would have been no more able to disturb my tranquillity with their plotting than they can trouble it henceforth with all their victories; let them enjoy my disgrace to the full, they will not prevent me from enjoying my innocence and finishing my days peacefully in spite of them.

Third Walk

Growing older, I learn all the time.

Solon often repeated this line in his old age. In a sense I could say the same, but the knowledge that the experience of twenty years has brought me is a poor thing, and even ignorance would be preferable. No doubt adversity is a great teacher, but its lessons are dearly bought, and often the profit we gain from them is not worth the price they cost us. What is more, these lessons come so late in the day that by the time we master them they are of no use to us. Youth is the time to study wisdom, age the time to practise it. Experience is always instructive, I admit, but it is only useful in the time we have left to live. When death is already at the door, is it worth learning how we should have lived?

What use to me are the insights I have gained so late and so painfully into my destiny and the passions of those who have made it what it is? If I have learned to know men better, it is only to feel more keenly the misery into which they have plunged me, nor has this knowledge, while laying bare all their traps, enabled me to avoid a single one. Why did I not remain in that foolish yet blessed faith, which made me for so many years the prey and plaything of my vociferous friends with never the least suspicion of all the plots enveloping me. I was their dupe and their victim, to be sure, but I believed they loved me, my heart enjoyed the friendship they had inspired in me, and I credited them with the same feelings. Those sweet illusions have been destroyed. The sad truth that time and reason have revealed to me in making me aware of my misfortune, has convinced me that there is no remedy and that resignation is my only course. Thus all the experience of my old age is of no use to me in my present state, nor will it help me in the future.

We enter the race when we are born and we leave it when we die. Why learn to drive your chariot better when you are close to the finishing post? All you have to consider then is how to make your exit. If an old man has something to learn, it is the art of dying, and this is precisely what occupies people least at my age; we think of anything rather than that. Old men are all more attached to life than children, and they leave it with a worse grace than the young. This is because all their labours have had this life in view, and at the end they see that it has all been in vain. When they go, they leave everything behind, all their concerns, all their goods, and the fruits of all their tireless endeavours. They have not thought to acquire anything during their lives that they could take with them when they die.

I told myself all this when there was still time, and if I have not been able to make better use of my reflections, this is not because they came too late or remained undigested. Thrown into the whirlpool of life while still a child, I learned from early experience that I was not made for this world, and that in it I would never attain the state to which my heart aspired. Ceasing therefore to seek among men the happiness which I felt I could never find there, my ardent imagination learned to leap over the boundaries of a life which was as yet hardly begun, as if it were flying over an alien land in search of a fixed and stable resting-place.

This desire, fostered by my early education and later strengthened by the long train of miseries and misfortunes that have filled my life, has at all times led me to seek after the nature and purpose of my being with greater interest and determination than I have seen in anyone else. I have met many men who were more learned in their philosophizing, but their philosophy remained as it were external to them. Wishing to know more than other people, they studied the workings of the universe, as they might have studied some machine they had come across, out of sheer curiosity. They studied human nature in order to speak knowledgeably about it, not in order to know themselves; their efforts were directed to the instruction of others and not to their own inner enlightenment. Several of them merely wanted to write a book, any book, so long as it was successful. Once it was written and published, its contents no longer interested them in the least. All they wanted was to have it accepted by other people and to defend it when it was attacked; beyond this they neither took anything from it for their own use nor concerned themselves with its truth or falsehood, provided it escaped refutation. For my part, when I have set out to learn something, my aim has been to gain knowledge for myself and not to be a teacher; I have always thought that before instructing others one should begin by knowing enough for one's own needs, and of all the studies I have undertaken in my life among men, there is hardly one that I would not equally have undertaken if I had been confined to a desert island for the rest of my days. What we ought to do depends largely on what we ought to believe, and in all matters other than the basic needs of our nature our opinions govern our actions. This principle, to which I have always adhered, has frequently led me to seek at length for the true purpose of my life so as to be able to determine its conduct, and feeling that this purpose was not to be found among men, I soon became reconciled to my incapacity for worldly success.

Born into a moral and pious family and brought up affectionately by a minister full of virtue and religion, I had received from my earliest years principles and maxims—prejudices, some might say—which have never entirely deserted me. While I was still a child, left to my own devices, led on by kindness, seduced by vanity, duped by hope and compelled by necessity, I became a Catholic, but I remained a Christian and soon my heart, under the influence of habit, became sincerely attached to my new religion. The instruction and good example I received from Madame de Warens confirmed me in this attachment. The rural solitude in which I spent the best days of my youth, and the reading of good books which completely absorbed me, strengthened my naturally affectionate tendencies in her company and led me to an almost Fénelon-like devotion. Lonely meditation, the study of nature and the contemplation of the universe lead the solitary to aspire continually to the maker of all things and to seek with a pleasing disquiet for the purpose of all he sees and the cause of all he feels. When my destiny cast me back into the torrent of this world, I found nothing there which could satisfy my heart for a single moment. Regret for the sweet liberty I had lost followed me everywhere and threw a veil of indifference or distaste over everything around me which might have brought me fame and fortune. Wavering in my uncertain desires, I hoped for little and obtained less, and even amidst the gleams of prosperity that came my way I felt that had I obtained all I thought I wanted, it would not have given me the happiness that my heart thirsted after without knowing clearly what it was. In this way everything conspired to detach my affections from this world, even before the onset of those misfortunes which were to make me a total stranger to it. I reached the age of forty, oscillating between poverty and riches, wisdom and error, full of vices born of habit, but with a heart free of evil inclinations, living at random with no rational principles, and careless but not scornful of my duties, of which I was often not fully aware.

Since the days of my youth I had fixed on the age of forty as the end of my efforts to succeed, the final term of my various ambitions. I had the firm intention, when I reached this age, of making no further effort to climb out of whatever situation I was in and of spending the rest of my life living from day to day with no thought for the future. When the time came I carried out my plan without difficulty, and although my fortune at that time seemed to be on the point of changing permanently for the better, it was not only without regret but with real pleasure that I gave up these prospects. In shaking off all these lures and vain hopes, I abandoned myself entirely to the nonchalant tranquillity which has always been my dominant taste and most lasting inclination. I quitted the world and its vanities, I gave up all finery—no more sword, no more watch, no more white stockings, gilt trimmings and powder, but a simple wig and a good solid coat of broadcloth—and what is more than all the rest, I uprooted from my heart the greed and covetousness which give value to all

I was leaving behind. I gave up the position I was then occupying, a position for which I was quite unsuited, and set myself to copying music at so much a page, an occupation for which I had always had a distinct liking.

I did not confine my reformation to outward things. Indeed I became aware that this change called for a revision of my opinions, which although undoubtedly more painful was also more necessary, and resolving to get it all over at once, I set about a strict self-examination which was to order my inner life for the rest of my days as I would wish it to be at the time of my death.

A great change which had recently come over me, a new moral vision of the world which had opened before me, the foolish judgements of men, whose absurdity I was beginning to sense without foreseeing how I was to fall victim to them, the ever-growing desire for something other than the literary celebrity which had hardly reached my nostrils before I was already sick of it, and finally the wish to find a less uncertain road for the rest of my career than that in which I had already spent the better half of it, all this impressed on me the long-felt need for such a general review of my opinions. I undertook it therefore, and neglected nothing in my power to carry it out successfully.

It is from this time that I can date my total renunciation of the world and the great love of solitude which has never since left me. The task I had set myself could only be performed in absolute isolation; it called for long and tranquil meditations which are impossible in the bustle of society life. So I was obliged to adopt for a time another way of life, which I subsequently found so much to my taste that since then I have only interrupted it for brief periods and against my will, returning to it most gladly and following it without effort as soon as I was able; and when men later reduced me to a life of solitude, I found that in isolating me to make me miserable, they had done more for my happiness than I had been able to do myself.

I set about the task I had undertaken with a zeal proportionate to the importance of the subject and its value to me. At this time I was living among certain modern philosophers who had little in common with the philosophers of antiquity. Instead of removing my doubts and curing my uncertainties they had shaken all my most assured beliefs concerning the questions which were most important to me, for these ardent missionaries of atheism, these overbearing dogmatists could not patiently endure that anyone should think differently from them on any subject whatsoever. I often defended myself rather feebly because of my distaste and lack of talent for disputation, but never once did I adopt their dismal teaching, and this resistance to such intolerant people, who had moreover their own ends in view, was not the least of the causes which sparked off their animosity towards me.

They had not persuaded me, but they had troubled me. Their arguments had shaken me without ever convincing me; I could not find the real answer to what they said, but I felt sure there must be one. I charged myself not so much with being mistaken as with being incompetent, and my heart answered them better than my reason.

Finally I said to myself: 'Shall I allow myself to be tossed eternally to and fro by the sophistries of the eloquent, when I am not even sure that the opinions they preach and press so ardently on others are really their own? Their passions, which determine their doctrine, and their interest in having this or that belief accepted, make it impossible to know what they themselves believe. Can one expect good faith from the leaders of parties? Their philosophy is meant for others; I need one for myself. Let me seek it with all my might while there is still time, so that I may have an assured rule of conduct for the rest of my days. I am now in the prime of life and the fullness of my mental powers. I am about to enter my decline. If I wait any longer, I shall no longer have all my powers to devote to my tardy deliberations, my intellectual faculties will have lost some of their vigour and I shall then do less well what today I can do as well as I ever shall; let me seize on this auspicious moment; it is the time of my outward and material reformation, let it also be the time of my intellectual and moral reformation. Let me decide my opinions and principles once and for all, and then let me remain for the rest of my life what mature consideration tells me I should be.'

I put this plan into effect slowly and haltingly, but I devoted to it all the effort and attention of which I was capable. I felt keenly that the tranquillity of the rest of my life and indeed my whole destiny depended on it. At the outset I found myself plunged into such a labyrinth of problems, difficulties, objections, complexities and obscurities that I was repeatedly tempted to abandon everything and was on the point of giving up my fruitless research and relying on the rules of common prudence in my deliberations without trying any further to find new rules in the principles which I had such difficulty in disentangling. But this prudence was itself so foreign to me and I felt so incapable of attaining it, that to take it for my guide would have been like searching through high seas and storms, without helm or compass, for a scarcely visible lantern which could never light my way to any port.

I persevered: for the first time in my life I acted courageously, and it is thanks to this success that I was able to withstand the horrible fate which was then beginning to envelop me without my having the least suspicion of it. After what were perhaps the most ardent and sincere investigations ever conducted by any mortal, I made up my mind once and for all on all the questions that concerned me, and if I was mistaken in my conclusions, I am sure at least that I cannot be blamed for my error since I did all I could to avoid it. It is true no doubt that the prejudices of childhood and the secret wishes of my heart tipped the scales on the side which was most comforting to me. It is hard to prevent oneself from believing what one so keenly desires, and who can doubt that the interest we have in admitting or denying the reality of the Judgement to come determines the faith of most men in accordance with their hopes and fears. All this may have led my reason astray, I admit, but it could not affect my good faith, for I was constantly in fear of error. If the use we made of this life was all that mattered, then it was important that I should know it, so as to be able to make the most of it while I still had time and not be a complete dupe. But what I feared most in the mood I was in, was to endanger the eternal fate of my soul for the sake of those worldly pleasures which have never seemed very precious to me.

I confess too that I did not always resolve to my own satisfaction all the difficulties which had perplexed me and which our philosophers had so often drummed into my ears. But having determined to make a final decision on matters which are so baffling to the human mind, and finding on all sides impenetrable mysteries and unanswerable objections, I adopted in every case the opinion which seemed to me the most clearly proved and the most credible in itself, without worrying about objections which I could not resolve, but which were met by other equally powerful objections in the opposing system. Only a charlatan will be dogmatic on such questions, but we must all have our own opinion and must choose it with all the maturity of judgement of which we are capable. If in spite of this we still fall far into error, we cannot in justice be held responsible for it, since we are not to blame. This is the unshakable principle on which I base my confidence.

The result of my arduous research was more or less what I have written down in my 'Profession of Faith of a Savoyard Priest', a work which has been ignobly prostituted and desecrated by the present generation, but which may one day effect a revolution in the minds of men, if ever good sense and good faith return among them.

Since then, remaining steadfast in the principles which I adopted after such long and careful meditation, I have made them the constant rule of my belief and conduct without wasting any further thought on the objections which I was unable to answer or on those which I had not foreseen and which arose from time to time in my mind. Sometimes they have worried me, but they have never shaken my faith. I have always said to myself: 'All these are hair-splitting metaphysical subtleties which count for nothing against the basic principles adopted by my reason, confirmed by my heart and bearing the seal of my conscience uninfluenced by passion. In matters so far above human understanding, shall I let an objection that I cannot answer overturn a whole body of doctrine which is so sound and coherent, the result of so much careful meditation, so well fitted to my reason, my heart and my whole being, and confirmed by that inner voice that I find absent from all the rest? No, empty logic-chopping will never destroy the close relation I perceive between my immortal nature and the constitution of the world, the physical order I see all around me. In the corresponding moral order, which my researches have brought to light, I find the support I need to be able to endure the miseries of my life. In any other system I should have no resources for living and no hope when dying. I should be the most unfortunate of creatures. Let us hold fast then to the only system which is able to make me happy in spite of fortune and my fellow-men.'

Do not these reflections and the conclusion I drew from them seem to have been sent down by Heaven itself to prepare me for the fate that awaited me and enable me to endure it? What would have become of me, what would become of me even now, in the terrible anguish that awaited me and in the unbelievable situation to which I am reduced for the rest of my days if, deprived of a refuge from my implacable persecutors, a consolation for the ignominy they force me to endure in this world, and a hope of obtaining one day the justice that is due to me, I had been abandoned entirely to the most horrible fate that a mortal has ever suffered on this earth? All the time when, untroubled in my innocence, I imagined that men felt nothing but benevolence and respect towards me and opened my frank and trusting heart to my friends and brothers, the traitors were silently ensnaring me in traps forged in the depths of hell. Taken unawares by this most unforeseen of misfortunes, the most terrible there is for a proud soul, trampled in the mire without knowing why or by whom, dragged into a pit of ignominy, enveloped in a horrible darkness through which I could make out nothing but sinister apparitions, I was overwhelmed by the first shock, and I should never have recovered from the prostration into which I was cast by the unexpectedness of this catastrophe, if I had not previously prepared the support I needed to struggle to my feet again.

It was only after years of anxiety, when I finally pulled myself together and began to be myself again, that I felt the value of the resources I had made ready against adversity. Having made up my mind on every question that concerned me, I saw, when I set my principles against the situation I was in, that I was giving far more than their real importance to the senseless judgments of men and the petty events of this brief life, that this life being merely a testing time, it mattered little what particular form of ordeal one encountered so long as the result was as it should be, and that therefore the greater, the more testing and the more numerous the ordeals, the more deserving it was to be able to endure them. All the sharpest torments lose their sting if one can confidently expect a glorious recompense, and the certainty of this recompense was the principal fruit of my earlier meditations.

It is true that in the midst of the unnumerable injuries and monstrous humiliations which were heaped on me from all sides, there were moments of doubt and anxiety when my faith was shaken and my peace disturbed. At such times the powerful objections which I had not been able to answer confronted my mind with renewed force and dealt me a final blow at precisely the moment when, overburdened by the weight of my destiny, I was on the point of giving way to discouragement. New arguments I heard would often return to reinforce those which had already tormented me. Then I would say to myself, my heart nearly bursting with agony: 'Oh, who can protect me from despair if in the horror of my fate I see nothing but fantasies in the consolation offered me by my own reason, if it can thus destroy its own work and overturn the edifice of hope and faith that it had built up in adversity! What help can I receive from illusions which deceive no one but me? The people of today see nothing but error and prejudice in the opinions in which I alone seek sustenance; in their eyes the truth is to be found in the system opposed to mine; they do not even seem able to believe that I have adopted mine in good faith, and I myself, even when I give myself over whole-heartedly to this faith, am faced by insurmountable difficulties that I cannot resolve. Yet I continue to believe in spite of them. Am I then the only wise man, the only man who has seen the light? Can I believe in an order of things simply because it suits me? Can I put an enlightened trust in appearances which lack all solidity in the eyes of my contemporaries and would seem illusory to me if my reason were not supported by my heart? Would it not have been better to combat my persecutors with their own weapons, adopting their principles rather than clinging to my own illusions, which I cannot defend against their onslaught?

23

I think myself wise, but I am a mere dupe, a victim and a martyr to an empty illusion.'

How often in these moments of doubt and uncertainty I was on the point of giving way to despair! If ever I had spent a whole month in this state, it would have been the end of me. But these crises, although once quite frequent, were always short-lived, and now, when I am still not quite free of them, they are so brief and infrequent that they have not even the power to disturb my peace of mind. They are mere flickers of anxiety which have no more effect on my soul than a feather falling into the water can have on the course of a river. I have realized that to raise again the points on which I had already made up my mind was to imagine that I had new insights or a better judgement or a greater desire for truth than at the time of my researches, and that since none of these was or could be the case with me, I could have no sound reason for preferring opinions which only tempted me so as to aggravate my unhappy state of despair, to opinions which I had adopted in the prime of life and the fullness of my mental powers, after the most profound consideration, and at a time when my untroubled life left me with no dominant interest other than that of discovering the truth. Today, when my heart is torn by anguish, my soul borne down by misery, my imagination clouded by fear and my head troubled by all the terrible mysteries that surround me, today when all my faculties have been enfeebled by age and care, shall I light-heartedly deprive myself of all the resources I had stored up for myself and place more trust in my declining reason, which makes me unjustly miserable, than in my mature and vigorous reason, which offers me a compensation for all my undeserved suffering?

No, I am neither wiser, nor better informed, nor more sincere than when I made up my mind on these important matters; I was well aware then of the objections which I allow to worry me today; they did not deter me then, and if some new and unforeseen difficulties have arisen, they are only the subtle sophistries of metaphysicians and cannot outweigh the eternal truths which have been accepted at all times and by all wise men, recognized by all nations, and indelibly engraved on the human heart. I knew, when I was pondering these things, that the human understanding, limited by the senses, could not fully comprehend them. I confined myself therefore to what was within my reach and did not attempt to understand what was beyond me. This was a reasonable course of action, I adopted it in the past and kept to it with the approval of my heart and my reason. What cause have I to abandon it at a time when so many powerful motives impel me to continue in it? What danger is there in following it? What would I gain from changing course? If I were to adopt the teaching of my persecutors, should I also adopt their morality—the rootless and sterile morality which they expound so grandiloquently in their books or with bravado in their plays but which never makes its way to the heart or the reason, or else the cruel secret morality, for which the other is only a mask, the esoteric doctrine of all their initiates which governs their behaviour and which they have so cleverly exercised at my expense? This morality is purely offensive, useless for self-defence and only good for attack. What use would it be to me in the state to which they have reduced

25

me? Only my innocence gives me strength in my misfortunes; how much more miserable I should be if I deprived myself of this single but powerful support and put malice in its place! Should I equal them in the art of mischief, and if I did, how would the harm I did them help me? I should lose my own self-respect and gain nothing in its place.

In this way, reasoning with myself, I was able to preserve my principles unshaken by specious arguments, insoluble objections and difficulties which lay beyond my reach and perhaps beyond that of the human mind. My own mind, resting on the most solid foundations I was able to provide, became so used to remaining there in the shelter of my conscience that no strange doctrine, old or new, can any longer disturb my peace for a single moment. Sunk in mental lethargy, I have forgotten the very arguments on which I based my belief and my principles, but I shall never forget the conclusions I drew from them with the approval of my conscience and my reason, and henceforth I shall never let them go. Let all the philosophers chop their logic against them; they will be wasting their time and their trouble. For the rest of my days I shall hold fast in all things to the position I adopted when I was better able to choose.

In this untroubled state of mind I find not only self-contentment, but the hope and consolation which my situation requires. A solitude so complete, so permanent and in itself so melancholy, the ever-present and constantly active animosity of all the present generation, the humiliations which they constantly heap on me, all this inevitably depresses me from time to time; uncertainty and worrying doubts still return occasionally to trouble my soul and fill it with gloom. Then it is that, being incapable of the thought processes which would be necessary to reassure myself, I feel the need to recall my former conclusions; I remember the painstaking attention and sincerity of heart which led me to them and all my confidence returns. Thus I reject all new ideas as fatal errors which have only a specious appearance of truth and are only fit to disturb my peace of mind.

In this way, confined to the narrow limits of my former knowledge, I have not, like Solon, the good fortune to learn all the time as I grow older; indeed I must refrain from the dangerous ambition of learning what I am no longer capable of knowing properly. But if I cannot hope to acquire much more in the way of useful knowledge, there is still much to be attained in the way of virtues necessary to my situation in life. Here it is that the time has come to enrich and adorn my soul with goods that it can carry with it when, set free of this body that obstructs and blinds it, it sees the truth face to face and comes to know the futility of all the knowledge which makes our false philosophers so vain. It will regret the moments wasted on attempts to acquire it in this life. But patience, kindness, resignation, integrity and impartial justice are goods that we can take with us and that we can accumulate continually without fear that death itself can rob us of their value. It is to this one useful study that I devote what remains of my old age. And I shall be happy if by my own self-improvement I learn to leave life, not better, for that is impossible, but more virtuous than when I entered it.

Fifth Walk

Of all the places where I have lived (and I have lived in some charming ones) none has made me so truly happy or left me such tender regrets as the Island of Saint-Pierre in the middle of the Lake of Bienne. This little island, which the people of Neuchâtel call the 'Île de la Motte', is scarcely known even in Switzerland. To my knowledge it has never yet been mentioned by any traveller. Yet it is very agreeable and wonderfully well situated for the happiness of those who like to live within narrow bounds—and even if I may be the only person ever to have had such a life thrust on him by destiny, I cannot believe that I am the only one to possess so natural a taste, though I have never yet encountered it in anyone else.

The shores of the Lake of Bienne are wilder and more romantic than those of Lake Geneva, since the rocks and woods come closer to the water, but they are no less pleasing. There may be fewer ploughed fields and vineyards, fewer towns and houses, but there is more natural greenery and there are more meadows and secluded spots shaded by woodlands, more frequent and dramatic changes of scenery. Since these happy shores are free of broad roads suitable for carriages, the region is little visited by travellers, but it is fascinating for those solitary dreamers who love to drink deeply of the beauty of nature and to meditate in a silence which is unbroken but for the cry of eagles, the occasional song of birds and the roar of streams cascading down from the mountains. In the middle of this beautiful, nearly circular expanse of water lie two small islands, one of them inhabited, cultivated and some half a league in circumference, the other one smaller, uninhabited, untilled, and bound one day to be eaten away by the constant removal of earth from it to make good the damage inflicted by waves and storms upon its neighbour. Thus it is that the substance of the poor always goes to enrich the wealthy.

There is only one house in the whole island, but it is a large, pleasant and commodious one, belonging like the island to the Hospital of Bern, and inhabited by a Steward together with his family and servants. He keeps a well-stocked farmyard, with fish-ponds and runs for game-birds. Small as it is, the island is so varied in soil and situation that it contains places suitable for crops of every kind. It includes fields, vineyards, woods, orchards, and rich pastures shaded by coppices and surrounded by shrubs of every variety, all of which are kept watered by the shores of the lake; on one shore an elevated terrace planted with two rows of trees runs the length of the island, and in the middle of this terrace there is a pretty summer-house where the people who live round the lake meet and dance on Sundays during the wine harvest.

It was on this island that I took refuge after the stoning at Môtiers. I found the place so delightful and so conducive to the life that suited me, that resolving to end my days there, I was concerned only lest I might not be allowed to carry out this plan, conflicting as it did with the scheme to carry me off to England, the first signs of which I was already beginning to detect. Troubled by forebodings, I could have desired that this place of refuge be made my lifelong prison, that I be shut up here for the rest of my days, deprived of any chance or hope of escaping and forbidden all communication with the mainland, so that not knowing what went on in the world, I should forget its existence and be forgotten by those who lived in it.

I was barely allowed to spend two months on this island, but I could have spent two years, two centuries and all eternity there without a moment's boredom, even though all the company I had, apart from Thérèse, was that of the Steward, his wife and his household—all certainly very good people, and nothing more, but this was exactly what I needed. I look upon these two months as the happiest time of my life, so happy that I would have been content to live all my life in this way, without a moment's desire for any other state.

What then was this happiness, and wherein lay this great contentment? The men of this age would never guess the answer from a description of the life I led there. Precious *far niente* was my first and greatest pleasure, and I set out to taste it in all its sweetness, and everything I did during my stay there was in fact no more than the delectable and necessary pastime of a man who has dedicated himself to idleness.

The hope that they would ask nothing better than to let me stay in the isolated place in which I had imprisoned myself, which I could not leave unaided and unobserved, and where I could have no communication or correspondence with the outside world except with the help of the people surrounding me, this hope encouraged me to hope likewise that I might end my days more peacefully than I had lived till then, and thinking that I would have all the time in the world to settle in, I began by making no attempt at all to install myself. Arriving there unexpectedly, alone and empty-handed, I sent in turn for my companion, my books and my few belongings, which I had the pleasure of leaving just as they were, unpacking not a single box or trunk and living in the house where I intended to end my days, as if it had been an inn which I was to leave the following day. Everything went along so well as it was that to try to order things better would have been to spoil them. One of my greatest joys was above all to leave my books safely shut up and to have no escritoire. When I was forced to take up my pen to answer the wretched letters I received, I reluctantly borrowed the Steward's escritoire and made haste to return it in the vain hope that I might never need to borrow it again. Instead of all these gloomy old papers and books, I filled my room with flowers and grasses, for I was then in the first flush of enthusiasm for botany, a taste soon to become a passion, which I owed to Doctor d'Ivernois. Not wanting to spend the time on serious work, I needed some agreeable pastime which would give me no more trouble than an idler likes to give himself. I set out to compose a *Flora Petrinsularis* and to describe every single plant on the island in enough detail to keep me busy for the rest of my days. They say a German once wrote a book about a lemon-skin; I could have written one about every grass in the meadows, every moss in the woods, every lichen covering the rocks—and I did not want to leave even one blade of grass or atom of vegetation without a full and detailed description. In accordance with this noble plan, every morning after breakfast, which we all took together, I would set out with a magnifying glass in my hand and my

Systema Naturae under my arm to study one particular section of the island, which I had divided for this purpose into small squares, intending to visit them all one after another in every season. Nothing could be more extraordinary than the raptures and ecstasies I felt at every discovery I made about the structure and organization of plants and the operation of the sexual parts in the process of reproduction, which was at this time completely new to me. Before progressing to rarer plants, I was delighted to observe in the common species the distinctions between families of which I had previously been completely unaware. The forking of the self-heal's two long stamens, the springiness of those of the nettle and wall pellitory, the way the seed bursts out from the fruit of the box and balsam, all these innumerable little tricks of fertilization which I was observing for the first time filled me with joy, and I went about asking people if they had seen the horns of the self-heal just as La Fontaine asked if they had read Habakkuk. After two or three hours I would come back with a rich harvest, enough to occupy me at home all the afternoon if it should rain. The rest of the morning I spent going with the Steward, his wife and Thérèse to see the labourers working at the harvest, and usually to lend them a hand; often people coming to see me from Bern found me perched up in a big tree with a bag round my waist, which I would fill with fruit and then lower to the ground on the end of a rope. My morning exercise and its attendant good humour made it very pleasant to take a rest at dinner-time, but when the meal went on too long and fine weather called me, I could not wait till the others had finished, and leaving them at table I would make my escape and install myself all alone in a boat,

32

which I would row out into the middle of the lake when it was calm; and there, stretching out full-length in the boat and turning my eyes skyward, I let myself float and drift wherever the water took me, often for several hours on end, plunged in a host of vague yet delightful reveries, which though they had no distinct or permanent subject, were still in my eyes infinitely to be preferred to all that I had found most sweet in the so-called pleasures of life. Often reminded by the declining sun that it was time to return home, I found myself so far from the island that I was forced to row with all my might in order to arrive before nightfall. At other times, rather than strike out into the middle of the lake, I preferred to stay close to the green shores of the island, where the clear water and cool shade often tempted me to bathe. But one of my most frequent expeditions was to go from the larger island to the smaller one, disembarking and spending the afternoon there, either walking in its narrow confines among the sallows, alders, persicarias and shrubs of all kinds, or else establishing myself on the summit of a shady hillock covered with turf, wild thyme and flowers, including even red and white clover which had probably been sown there at some time in the past, a perfect home for rabbits, which could multiply there in peace, without harming anything or having anything to fear. I put the idea to the Steward, who sent for rabbits from Neuchâtel, both bucks and does, and we proceeded in great ceremony, his wife, one of his sisters, Thérèse and I, to install them on the little island, where they were beginning to breed before my departure and where they will doubtless have flourished if they have been able to withstand the rigours of winter. The founding of this little colony was a great day. The pilot of the Argonauts was not prouder than I was, when I led the company and the rabbits triumphantly from the large island to the small one; and I was gratified to see that the Steward's wife, who was extremely afraid of water and could not step into a boat without feeling unwell, embarked confidently under my command and showed no sign of fear during the crossing.

When the lake was not calm enough for boating, I would spend the afternoon roaming about the island, stopping to sit now in the most charming and isolated corners where I could dream undisturbed, and now on the terraces and little hills, where I could let my eyes wander over the beautiful and entrancing spectacle of the lake and its shores, crowned on one side by the near-by mountains and on the other extending in rich and fertile plains where the view was limited only by a more distant range of blue mountains.

As evening approached, I came down from the heights of the island, and I liked then to go and sit on the shingle in some secluded spot by the edge of the lake; there the noise of the waves and the movement of the water, taking hold of my senses and driving all other agitation from my soul, would plunge it into a delicious reverie in which night often stole upon me unawares. The ebb and flow of the water, its continuous yet undulating noise, kept lapping against my ears and my eyes, taking the place of all the inward movements which my reverie had calmed within me, and it was enough to make me pleasurably aware of my existence, without troubling myself with thought. From time to time some brief and insubstantial reflection arose concerning the instability of the things of this world, whose image I saw in the surface of

34

the water, but soon these fragile impressions gave way before the unchanging and ceaseless movement which lulled me and without any active effort on my part occupied me so completely that even when time and the habitual signal called me home I could hardly bring myself to go.

After supper, when the evening was fine, we all went out once again to walk on the terrace and breathe the coolness of the lake air. We would sit down to rest in the summer-house, and laugh and talk, and sing some old song which was fully the equal of all our modern frills and fancies, and then we would go off to bed satisfied with our day and only wishing for the next day to be the same.

Such, apart from unforeseen and troublesome visits, was the way I spent my time on this island during the weeks I lived there. I should like to know what there was in it that was attractive enough to give me such deep, tender and lasting regrets that even fifteen years later I am incapable of thinking of this beloved place without being overcome by pangs of longing.

I have noticed in the changing fortunes of a long life that the periods of the sweetest joys and keenest pleasures are not those whose memory is most moving and attractive to me. Those brief moments of madness and passion, however powerfully they may affect us, can because of this very power only be infrequent points along the line of our life. They are too rare and too short-lived to constitute a durable state, and the happiness for which my soul longs is not made up of fleeting moments, but of a single and lasting state, which has no very strong impact in itself, but which by its continuance becomes so captivating that we eventually come to regard it as the height of happiness.

Everything is in constant flux on this earth. Nothing keeps the same unchanging shape, and our affections, being attached to things outside us, necessarily change and pass away as they do. Always out ahead of us or lagging behind, they recall a past which is gone or anticipate a future which may never come into being; there is nothing solid there for the heart to attach itself to. Thus our earthly joys are almost without exception the creatures of a moment; I doubt whether any of us knows the meaning of lasting happiness. Even in our keenest pleasures there is scarcely a single moment of which the heart could truthfully say: 'Would that this moment could last for ever!' And how can we give the name of happiness to a fleeting state which leaves our hearts still empty and anxious, either regretting something that is past or desiring something that is yet to come?

But if there is a state where the soul can find a resting-place secure enough to establish itself and concentrate its entire being there, with no need to remember the past or reach into the future, where time is nothing to it, where the present runs on indefinitely but this duration goes unnoticed, with no sign of the passing of time, and no other feeling of deprivation or enjoyment, pleasure or pain, desire or fear than the simple feeling of existence, a feeling that fills our soul entirely, as long as this state lasts, we can call ourselves happy, not with a poor, incomplete and relative happiness such as we find in the pleasures of life, but with a sufficient, complete and perfect happiness which leaves no emptiness to be filled in the soul. Such is the state which I often experienced on the Island of Saint-Pierre in my solitary reveries, whether I lay in a boat and drifted where the water carried me, or sat by the shores of the stormy lake, or elsewhere, on the banks of a lovely river or a stream murmuring over the stones.

What is the source of our happiness in such a state? Nothing external to us, nothing apart from ourselves and our own existence; as long as this state lasts we are self-sufficient like God. The feeling of existence unmixed with any other emotion is in itself a precious feeling of peace and contentment which would be enough to make this mode of being loved and cherished by anyone who could guard against all the earthly and sensual influences that are constantly distracting us from it in this life and troubling the joy it could give us. But most men being continually stirred by passion know little of this condition, and having only enjoyed it fleetingly and incompletely they retain no more than a dim and confused notion of it and are unaware of its true charm. Nor would it be desirable in our present state of affairs that the avid desire for these sweet ecstasies should give people a distaste for the active life which their constantly recurring needs impose upon them. But an unfortunate man who has been excluded from human society, and can do nothing more in this world to serve or benefit himself or others, may be allowed to seek in this state a compensation for human joys, a compensation which neither fortune nor mankind can take away from him.

It is true that such compensations cannot be experienced by every soul or in every situation. The heart must be at peace and its calm untroubled by any passion. The person in question must be suitably disposed and the surrounding objects conducive to his happiness. There must be neither a total calm nor too much movement, but a steady and moderate motion, with no jolts or breaks. Without any movement life is mere lethargy. If the movement is irregular or too violent it arouses us from our dreams; recalling us to an awareness of the surrounding objects, it destroys the charm of reverie and tears us from our inner self, bowing us once again beneath the yoke of fortune and mankind and reviving in us the sense of our misfortunes. Complete silence induces melancholy; it is an image of death. In such cases the assistance of a happy imagination is needed, and it comes naturally to those whom Heaven has blessed with it. The movement which does not come from outside us arises within us at such times. Our tranquillity is less complete, it is true, but it is also more agreeable when pleasant and insubstantial ideas barely touch the surface of the soul, so to speak, and do not stir its depths. One needs only enough of such ideas to allow one to be conscious of one's existence while forgetting all one's troubles. This type of reverie can be enjoyed anywhere where one is undisturbed, and I have often thought that in the Bastille, and even in a dungeon with not a single object to rest my eyes on, I could still have dreamed pleasantly.

But it must be admitted that this happened much more easily and agreeably in a fertile and lonely island, naturally circumscribed and cut off from the rest of the world, where I saw nothing but images of delight, where there was nothing to recall painful memories, where the company of the few people who lived there was attractive and pleasing without being interesting enough to absorb all my attention, and where I could devote the whole day without care of hindrance to the pastimes of my choice or to the most blissful indolence. It was without doubt a fine opportunity for a dreamer who is capable of enjoying the most delightful fantasies even in the most unpleasant settings, and who could here feed on them at leisure, enriching them with all the objects which his senses actually perceived. Emerging from a long and happy reverie, seeing myself surrounded by greenery, flowers and birds, and letting my eyes wander over the picturesque far-off shores which enclosed a vast stretch of clear and crystalline water, I fused my imaginings with these charming sights, and finding myself in the end gradually brought back to myself and my surroundings, I could not draw a line between fiction and reality; so much did everything conspire equally to make me love the contemplative and solitary life I led in that beautiful place. Would that it could come again! Would that I could go and end my days on that beloved island, never leaving it nor seeing again any inhabitants of the mainland who might recall the memory of the calamities of every kind which it has been their pleasure to heap upon me for so many years! They would soon be forgotten for ever; of course they might not similarly forget me, but what could that matter to me, so long as they were kept from troubling my quiet retreat? Set free from all the earthly passions that are born of the tumult of social life, my soul would often soar out of this atmosphere and would converse before its time with the celestial spirits whose number it hopes soon to swell. I know that mankind will never let me return to this happy sanctuary, where they did not allow me to remain. But at least they cannot prevent me from being transported there every day on the wings of imagination and tasting for several hours the same pleasures as if I were still living there. Were I there, my sweetest occupation would be to dream to my heart's content. Is it not the same thing to dream that I am there? Better still, I can add to my abstract and monotonous reveries charming images that give them life. During my moments of ecstasy the sources of these images often escaped my senses; but now, the deeper the reverie, the more vividly they are present to me. I am often more truly in their midst and they give me still greater pleasure than when I was surrounded by them. My misfortune is that as my imagination loses its fire this happens less easily and does not last so long. Alas, it is when we are beginning to leave this mortal body that it most offends us!

Eighth Walk

Meditating on my state of mind in all the various circumstances of my life, I am extremely struck by the lack of proportion between the ups and downs of my fate and the general feelings of well-being or dejection they have aroused in me. The various periods of short-lived prosperity that I have enjoyed have left me with almost no agreeable memories of deep and lasting impressions: by contract, in all the hardships of my life I was invariably full of affectionate, touching and delightful emotions which poured a healing balm over the wounds of my injured soul and seemed to change its pains into pleasures, and it is the sweet memory of these feelings that returns to me, unaccompanied by that of the adversities which I experienced at the same time. It seems to me that I enjoyed the pleasure of existence more completely and that I lived more fully when my emotions were so to speak concentrated around my heart by my destiny and could not go spreading themselves over all the things prized by men, things that are of so little value in themselves, though they form the sole occupation of the people we regard as happy.

When all was in order round about me and I was happy with everything surrounding me and with the sphere in which I had to live, I filled it with my affections. My expansive soul spread to encompass other objects, and I was all the time transported outside myself by a thousand different tastes and by pleasing attachments which kept my heart constantly occupied, so that I could be said to have forgotten myself. My entire being was in things that were foreign to me, and in the continual agitation of my heart I felt all the instability of human life. This stormy life gave me neither inward peace nor outward repose. Happy to all appearances, I had not a single feeling which could stand the test of thought and with which I could feel entirely at ease. I was never completely satisfied with others or with myself. I was deafened by the tumult of the world and bored by solitude, I was always wanting to move and never happy anywhere. And yet I was acclaimed, made much of, and welcomed with open arms. I had not a single enemy, no one who was malevolently or enviously disposed towards me. Since people's one concern was to shower favours on me, I often had the pleasure of doing favours in my turn, and to a great many people, so that with neither possessions, nor a position in the world, nor a patron, nor any great abilities that had had time to develop or become known, I enjoyed the advantages attached to such things and could see no one either above or below me whose situation I envied. What then did I need to make me happy? I do not know, but I know that I was not happy. And what is missing now to make me the most unfortunate of men? Nothing that mankind could do. Yet even so, in these deplorable circumstances, I would not change places with the most fortunate of my fellow-men, and I would rather be myself with all my misfortunes than one of them in all his prosperity. Reduced to my own self, it is true that I feed on my own substance, but this does not diminish and I can be self-sufficient even though I have to ruminate as it were on nothing, and though my dried-up imagination and inactive mind no longer provide my heart with any nourishment. My soul, darkened and encumbered by my bodily organs, sinks daily beneath their weight; bowed under this heavy burden, it no longer has the strength to soar as once it did above this old integument.

Adversity forces us to draw in on ourselves in this way, and this is perhaps what makes it most difficult to bear for most people. For my part, since I have only errors to reproach myself with, I can console myself by blaming them on my weakness, for premeditated evil never came near my heart.

Nevertheless, short of being totally insensible, how is it possible to contemplate my situation for a single instant without seeing how horrible they have made it, without dying of grief and despair? On the contrary, I, the most sensitive of beings, contemplate it unmoved, and without having to struggle or force myself, I can look on my situation with near-indifference when hardly anyone else could consider it without being appalled.

How has this come about? For I was far removed from this peaceful frame of mind when I first came to suspect the plot in which I had long been unwittingly ensnared. I was overwhelmed by this new discovery. The infamy and treachery of it took me by surprise. What honest soul is prepared for sufferings of this kind? To be able to foresee them, one would need to have deserved them. I fell into all the pits that had been dug for me. Indignation, fury and frenzy took possession of me. I lost my bearings. My wits were unsettled, and in the horrible darkness in which they have kept me buried, I could see no light to guide me, no support or foothold to keep me upright and help me to resist the despair that was engulfing me.

How could one live a quiet and happy life in such circumstances? Yet the circumstances have not changed, or they have changed for the worse, and I have regained my peace and tranquillity and lead a quiet and happy life in the midst of them, laughing at the incredible tortures my persecutors are constantly inflicting on themselves while I live in peace, busy with flowers, stamens and such childish things, and never giving them a moment's thought.

How did this change take place? By a natural, imperceptible and painless process. The initial shock was terrible. I, who felt myself worthy of affection and respect, who thought myself honoured and loved as I deserved to be, suddenly found myself disguised as an unheard of and fearful monster. I saw a whole generation all rush headlong into this strange belief, without explanation, doubt or shame, and without my even being able to discover the cause of this extraordinary turn of events. I struggled violently and succeeded only in enmeshing myself still further. I tried to force my persecutors to have it out with me in public; they took good care to do no such thing. After tormenting myself for a long time, I was bound to stop and draw breath. But I still hoped: I said to myself: 'The whole of the human race can never be infected by this idiotic blindness, this absurd prejudice. There are sensible people who do not share in this madness; there are equitable souls who detest treachery and deceit. Let me look, I shall perhaps finish by finding a man, and if I find one, they will all be confounded.' I sought in vain; I did not find one single man. It is a universal league, irrevocable and without exception, and I can be certain of ending my days in this terrible ostracism without ever unravelling the mystery.

It is in this deplorable situation that after years of anguish I have escaped from the despair which seemed to be my ultimate lot, and recovered my serenity, tranquillity, peace and even happiness, since every day of my life brings a pleasurable recollection of the last and no desire for anything different in the one to come.

What has brought about this change? One thing and one thing only: I have learned to bear the yoke of necessity without complaining. Where previously I strove to cling on to a host of things, now, when I have lost hold of them all one after another and have nothing left but myself, I have at last regained a firm footing. Under pressure from all sides, I remain upright because I cling to nothing and lean on myself.

When I used to protest so fiercely against public opinion, I was still its slave without realizing it. We want to be respected by those whom we respect, and as long as I thought well of men, or at least of certain men, I could not remain indifferent to their opinion of me. I saw that the judgements of the public are often fair, but I did not see that this very fairness is often the work of chance, that the criteria on which men base their opinions are merely the fruit of their passions or of the prejudices which spring from these passions, and that even when they judge correctly, this often has an unjust cause, as when they pretend to honour the merits of a successful man not out of fairness, but to give themselves an appearance of impartiality, while they are quite prepared to slander this same person in other ways.

But when after a long and fruitless search I saw that they all without exception remained attached to the most iniquitous and absurd theory that a spirit from Hell could ever have invented, when I saw that where I was concerned reason was banished from every mind and justice from every heart, when I saw a frenzied generation give itself over entirely to the blind fury of its leaders against an unfortunate individual who never harmed anyone, never wished anyone ill and never rendered evil for evil, when after vainly seeking a man I had finally to put out my lantern exclaiming; 'There is not a single one left,' then I began to see that I was alone in the world, and I understood that my contemporaries acted towards me like automata, entirely governed by external impulses, and that I could only calculate their behaviour according to the laws of motion. Any intention or passion that I might have supposed them to possess could never have provided an intelligible explanation of their conduct towards me. Thus it was that their inner feelings ceased to matter to me; I came to see them as no more than bodies endowed with different movements, but devoid of any moral relation to me.

In all the ills that befall us, we are more concerned by the intention than the result. A tile that falls off a roof may injure us more seriously, but it will not wound us so deeply as a stone thrown deliberately by a malevolent hand. The blow may miss, but the intention always strikes home. The physical pain is what we feel least of all when fortune assails us, and when suffering people do not know whom to blame for their misfortunes, they attribute them to a destiny, and personify this destiny, lending it eyes and a mind that takes plea-

46

sure in tormenting them. In the same way a gambler who is angered by his losses will fly into a fury against some unknown enemy; he imagines a fate which deliberately persists in torturing him, and having found something to feed his anger on, he storms and rages against the enemy that he has himself created. The wise man sees in all his misfortunes no more than the blows of blind necessity and feels none of this senseless agitation; his pain makes him cry out, but without anger or exasperation, he feels only the physical impact of the evil that besets him, and though the blows may hurt his body, not one of them can touch his heart.

To have come so far is excellent, but it is not enough if one stops there. That would be like cutting down the evil, but leaving the root in the ground, for this root is not in beings outside us, but in ourselves, and that is where we must exert ourselves to pull it out completely. This became obvious to me when once I had begun to be myself again. Since by the light of reason I could see nothing but absurdities in the explanations I tried to give for everything that happened to me, I realized that, as all its causes and operations were unknown and incomprehensible to me, I should ignore them completely, that I should regard all the details of my fate as the workings of mere necessity, in which I should not seek to find any intention, purpose, or moral cause, that I must submit to it without argument or resistance since these were useless, that since all that was left to me on earth was to regard myself as a purely passive being, I should not waste the strength I needed to endure my fate in trying to fight against it. This was what I told myself. My reason and my heart assented, yet I could feel that my heart was not entirely satis-

47

fied. Whence came this dissatisfaction? I searched and found the answer: it came from my self-love, which, having waxed indignant against mankind, still rebelled against reason.

This discovery was not as easy as one might believe, for an innocent and persecuted man is all too inclined to mistake his own petty pride for a pure love of justice, but on the other hand, once the real cause is found, it is easy to remedy, or at least to deflect to another course. Self-esteem is the strongest impulse of proud souls; self-love, with its train of illusions, can often creep in under the guise of self-esteem, but when the fraud is finally revealed and self-love can no longer conceal itself, there is no further cause to fear it, and though it may be hard to destroy, at least it is easy to subdue.

I was never much given to self-love; but in the world this artificial passion has been exacerbated in me, particularly when I was a writer; I may perhaps have had less of it than my fellow-authors, but it was still excessive. The terrible lessons I received quickly reduced it to its original proportions. At first it rebelled against injustice, but in the end it came to treat it with contempt; falling back on my own soul, severing the external links which make it so demanding, and giving up all ideas of comparison or precedence, it was content that I be good in my own eyes. And so, becoming once again the proper love of self, it returned to the true natural order and freed me from the tyranny of public opinion.

From this time on I recovered my peace of mind and something akin to happiness. Whatever our situation, it is only self-love that can make us constantly unhappy. When it is silent and we listen to the voice of reason, this can console us in the end for all the misfortunes which it was not in our power to avoid. Indeed it makes them disappear, in so far as they have no immediate effect on us, for one can be sure of avoiding their worst buffets by ceasing to take any notice of them. They are as nothing to the person who ignores them. Insults, reprisals, offences, injuries, injustices are all nothing to the man who sees in the hardships he suffers nothing but the hardships themselves and not the intention behind them, and whose place in his own self-esteem does not depend on the good-will of others. However men choose to regard me, they cannot change my essential being, and for all their power and all their secret plots I shall continue, whatever they do, to be what I am in spite of them. It is true that their attitude towards me has an influence on my material situation. The wall they have set up between us robs me of every source of subsistence or assistance in my old age and my time of need. It makes even money useless to me, since money cannot buy the help I need, and there is no intercourse, no mutual aid, no communication between us. Alone in their midst, I have only myself to fall back on, and this is a feeble support at my age and in my situation. These are great misfortunes, but they are no longer so painful to me now that I have learned to endure them patiently. There are not many things that we really need. Forethought and imagination multiply their number, and it is these unceasing cares which make us anxious and unhappy. But I, even if I know that I shall suffer tomorrow, can be content as long as I am not suffering today. I am not affected by the ills I foresee, but only by those I feel, and this reduces them to very little. Solitary, sick, and left alone in my bed, I could die there of poverty, cold and hunger without anyone caring. But what does it matter if I myself do not care and am no more affected than the rest of them by my fate, whatever it may be? Is it such a small achievement, particularly at my age, to have learned to regard life and death, sickness and health, riches and poverty, fame and slander with equal indifference? All other old men worry about everything, nothing worries me. Whatever may happen, I do not care, and this indifference is not the work of my own wisdom, it is that of my enemies and compensates me for the evils they inflict upon me. In making me insensible to adversity they have done me more good than if they had spared me its blows. If I did not experience it I might still fear it, but now that I have subdued it I have no more cause to fear.

In the midst of my afflictions this disposition gives free rein to my natural nonchalance almost as completely as if I were living in the most total prosperity. Apart from the brief moments when the objects around me recall my most painful anxieties, all the rest of the time, following the promptings of my natural affections, my heart continues to feed on the emotions for which it was created, and I enjoy them together with the imaginary beings who provoke them and share them with me, just as if those beings really existed. They exist for me, their creator, and I have no fear that they will betray or abandon me; they will last as long as my misfortunes and will suffice to make me forget them.

Everything brings me back to the sweet and happy life for which I was born; I spend three-quarters of my life either busy with instructive and even pleasant objects, to which it is a joy to devote my mind and my senses, or with the children of my imagination, the creatures of my heart's desire, whose presence satisfies its yearnings, or else alone with myself, contented with myself and already enjoying the happiness which I feel I have deserved. Love of self alone is active in all of this, self-love has no part in it. The same is not true during those unhappy moments which I still spend among men, a plaything of their Judas kisses, their extravagant and hollow compliments and their honeyed malice. For all my efforts, self-love steps in on such occasions. I suffer agonies from the hate and animosity I see in their hearts under such crude disguises, and in addition to this pain the idea of being duped in such a silly way causes me a childish resentment, the product of a foolish self-love whose stupidity I can see all too clearly without being able to suppress it. The efforts I have made to harden myself against these insulting and mocking looks are unbelievable. A hundred times I have walked in public places and on the busiest thoroughfares with the sole object of learning to put up with these cruel looks; not only was I unable to do so, I did not even make any progress and all my painful and fruitless efforts left me just as vulnerable as before to being upset, hurt or exasperated.

Governed by my senses whether I like it or not, I have never been able to resist the impressions they make on me, and as long as they are affected by some object my heart remains equally affected, but this passing emotion lasts no longer than the sensations that cause it. The presence of people who hate me affects me violently, but as soon as they disappear the emotion ceases; out of sight, out of mind. Even when I know that they are going to concern themselves with me, I am unable to concern myself with them. The suffering which I no longer actually feel has not the slightest effect on me; the persecutor whom I cannot see is as nothing to me. I can see what an advantage this gives to those who control my destiny. Let them control it as they please. I would rather be exposed to all their torments than be obliged to think about them in order to protect myself from their attacks.

This influence of my senses on my heart is my one torment in life. On the days when I see no one, I give no thought to my fate, I am no longer conscious of it and I do not suffer; I live happy and contented with nothing to distract or hinder me. But it is not often that I can avoid all painful impressions, and when such things are furthest from my mind I notice some gesture or sinister look, overhear some barbed remark or meet some malicious person, and this is enough to upset me completely. All I can do in such circumstances is to forget as quickly as I can and run away. The turmoil in my heart vanishes with the object that has caused it and calm descends on my soul again as soon as I am alone. Or if anything does worry me, it is the fear of meeting some new cause of suffering. This is my only source of distress, but it is enough to spoil my happiness. I live in the middle of Paris. When I leave my home, I long for solitude and the country, but they are so far away that before I can breath freely I have to encounter a thousand things that oppress my heart, and half the day goes by in anguish before I reach the refuge I am looking for. Indeed, I am lucky to be allowed to get there. The movement when I escape from the horde of evil-doers is one of joy, and as soon as I am under the trees and surrounded by greenery, I feel as if I were in the earthly paradise and experience an inward pleasure as intense as if I were the happiest of men.

I well remember how in my brief periods of prosperity these same solitary walks which give me such pleasure today were tedious and insipid to me. When I was staying with someone in the country the need for exercise and fresh air often led me to go walking by myself, and I would sneak out like a thief and wander through the park or the countryside, but far from enjoying the quiet happiness that I find there today, I took with me the turmoil of futile ideas which had occupied me in the salon; the memory of the company I had left followed me in my solitude, the fumes of self-love and the bustle of the world dimmed the freshness of the groves in my eyes and troubled my secluded peace. Though I fled into the depths of the woods, an importunate crowd followed me everywhere and came between me and Nature. Only when I had detached myself from the social passions and their dismal train did I find her once again in all her beauty.

Convinced of the impossibility of repressing these first involuntary reactions, I have given up the attempt. Whenever I am provoked, I allow my blood to boil and my senses to be possessed by anger and indignation; I give way to this first explosion of nature, which all my efforts could not prevent or impede. I merely try to stop it leading to any undesirable consequences. My eyes flash, my face flares up, my limbs tremble and palpitations choke me; these are all purely physical reactions and reasoning has no effect on them, but once nature has had this initial explosion one can become one's own master again and gradually regain control over one's senses; this is what I have tried to do, for a long time to no avail, but eventually with greater success. And instead of wasting my efforts on pointless resistance, I wait for the moment when I can achieve victory by appealing to my reason, for it only speaks when it can make itself heard. Alas! What am I saying? My reason? It would be quite wrong of me to attribute this victory to reason, for it has little to do with it; all my behaviour is equally the work of a volatile temperament which is stirred up by violent winds but calms down as soon as the winds stop blowing; it is the ardour of my character that excites me and the nonchalance of my character that pacifies me. I give way to the impulse of the moment; every shock sets up a vigorous and short lived motion in me, but as soon as the shock is over the motion vanishes, and nothing that comes from outside can be prolonged within me. All the vicissitudes of fortune and the stratagems of men can have little hold on a man of my kind. For the suffering to last the external cause would have to be constantly renewed, because any interval, however short, is enough for me to regain my self-control. I am at men's mercy as long as they can act on my senses, but they have only to grant me a moment's respite for me to revert to my natural state; whatever men may do, this is my most enduring state and the one in which, in spite of destiny, I enjoy the kind of happiness for which I feel I was made. I have described this state in one of my reveries. It suits me so well that I desire nothing other than that it should continue and never be disturbed. The evil that men have done me does not affect me in the least; only the fear of what they may still do to me is capable of disquieting me, but being certain that there is no new hold which they can use to inflict some permanent suffering on me, I laugh at all their scheming and enjoy my own existence in spite of them.

PENGUIN 60S CLASSICS

APOLLONIUS OF RHODES · *Jason and the Argonauts*
ARISTOPHANES · *Lysistrata*
SAINT AUGUSTINE · *Confessions of a Sinner*
JANE AUSTEN · *The History of England*
HONORÉ DE BALZAC · *The Atheist's Mass*
BASHŌ · *Haiku*
AMBROSE BIERCE · *An Occurrence at Owl Creek Bridge*
JAMES BOSWELL · *Meeting Dr Johnson*
CHARLOTTE BRONTË · *Mina Laury*
CAO XUEQIN · *The Dream of the Red Chamber*
THOMAS CARLYLE · *On Great Men*
BALDESAR CASTIGLIONE · *Etiquette for Renaissance Gentlemen*
CERVANTES · *The Jealous Extremaduran*
KATE CHOPIN · *The Kiss and Other Stories*
JOSEPH CONRAD · *The Secret Sharer*
DANTE · *The First Three Circles of Hell*
CHARLES DARWIN · *The Galapagos Islands*
THOMAS DE QUINCEY · *The Pleasures and Pains of Opium*
DANIEL DEFOE · *A Visitation of the Plague*
BERNAL DÍAZ · *The Betrayal of Montezuma*
FYODOR DOSTOYEVSKY · *The Gentle Spirit*
FREDERICK DOUGLASS · *The Education of Frederick Douglass*
GEORGE ELIOT · *The Lifted Veil*
GUSTAVE FLAUBERT · *A Simple Heart*
BENJAMIN FRANKLIN · *The Means and Manner of Obtaining Virtue*
EDWARD GIBBON · *Reflections on the Fall of Rome*
CHARLOTTE PERKINS GILMAN · *The Yellow Wallpaper*
GOETHE · *Letters from Italy*
HOMER · *The Rage of Achilles*
HOMER · *The Voyages of Odysseus*

PENGUIN 60S CLASSICS

HENRY JAMES · *The Lesson of the Master*
FRANZ KAFKA · *The Judgement* and *In the Penal Colony*
THOMAS À KEMPIS · *Counsels on the Spiritual Life*
HEINRICH VON KLEIST · *The Marquise of O—*
LIVY · *Hannibal's Crossing of the Alps*
NICCOLÒ MACHIAVELLI · *The Art of War*
SIR THOMAS MALORY · *The Death of King Arthur*
GUY DE MAUPASSANT · *Boule de Suif*
FRIEDRICH NIETZSCHE · *Zarathustra's Discourses*
OVID · *Orpheus in the Underworld*
PLATO · *Phaedrus*
EDGAR ALLAN POE · *The Murders in the Rue Morgue*
ARTHUR RIMBAUD · *A Season in Hell*
JEAN-JACQUES ROUSSEAU · *Meditations of a Solitary Walker*
ROBERT LOUIS STEVENSON · *Dr Jekyll and Mr Hyde*
TACITUS · *Nero and the Burning of Rome*
HENRY DAVID THOREAU · *Civil Disobedience* and *Reading*
LEO TOLSTOY · *The Death of Ivan Ilyich*
IVAN TURGENEV · *Three Sketches from a Hunter's Album*
MARK TWAIN · *The Man That Corrupted Hadleyburg*
GIORGIO VASARI · *Lives of Three Renaissance Artists*
EDITH WHARTON · *Souls Belated*
WALT WHITMAN · *Song of Myself*
OSCAR WILDE · *The Portrait of Mr W. H.*

ANONYMOUS WORKS

Beowulf and Grendel
Buddha's Teachings
Gilgamesh and Enkidu

Krishna's Dialogue on the Soul
Tales of Cú Chulaind
Two Viking Romances

READ MORE IN PENGUIN

For complete information about books available from Penguin and how to order them, please write to us at the appropriate address below. Please note that for copyright reasons the selection of books varies from country to country.

IN THE UNITED KINGDOM: Please write to *Dept. JC, Penguin Books Ltd, FREEPOST, West Drayton, Middlesex UB7 0BR.*

If you have any difficulty in obtaining a title, please send your order with the correct money, plus ten per cent for postage and packaging, to *PO Box No. 11, West Drayton, Middlesex UB7 0BR.*

IN THE UNITED STATES: Please write to *Consumer Sales, Penguin USA, P.O. Box 999, Dept. 17109, Bergenfield, New Jersey 07621-0120.* VISA and MasterCard holders call 1-800-253-6476 to order all Penguin titles.

IN CANADA: Please write to *Penguin Books Canada Ltd, 10 Alcorn Avenue, Suite 300, Toronto, Ontario M4V 3B2.*

IN AUSTRALIA: Please write to *Penguin Books Australia Ltd, P.O. Box 257, Ringwood, Victoria 3134.*

IN NEW ZEALAND: Please write to *Penguin Books (NZ) Ltd, Private Bag 102902, North Shore Mail Centre, Auckland 10.*

IN INDIA: Please write to *Penguin Books India Pvt Ltd, 706 Eros Apartments, 56 Nehru Place, New Delhi 110 019.*

IN THE NETHERLANDS: Please write to *Penguin Books Netherlands bv, Postbus 3507, NL-1001 AH Amsterdam.*

IN GERMANY: Please write to *Penguin Books Deutschland GmbH, Metzlerstrasse 26, 60594 Frankfurt am Main.*

IN SPAIN: Please write to *Penguin Books S. A., Bravo Murillo 19, 1o B, 28015 Madrid.*

IN ITALY: Please write to *Penguin Italia s.r.l., Via Felice Casati 20, I-20124 Milano.*

IN FRANCE: Please write to *Penguin France S. A., 17 rue Lejeune, F-31000 Toulouse.*

IN JAPAN: Please write to *Penguin Books Japan, Ishikiribashi Building, 2-5-4, Suido, Bunkyo-ku, Tokyo 112.*

IN GREECE: Please write to *Penguin Hellas Ltd, Dimocritou 3, GR-106 71 Athens.*

IN SOUTH AFRICA: Please write to *Longman Penguin Southern Africa (Pty) Ltd, Private Bag X08, Bertsham 2013.*